What readers are saying about IN 30 MINUTES® guides:

Google Drive & Docs In 30 Minutes

"I bought your Google Docs guide myself (my new company uses it) and it was really handy. I loved it."

"I have been impressed by the writing style and how easy it was to get very familiar and start leveraging Google Docs. I can't wait for more titles. Nice job!"

Genealogy Basics In 30 Minutes

"This basic genealogy book is a fast, informative read that will get you on your way if you are ready to begin your genealogy journey or are looking for tips to push past a problem area."

"The personal one-on-one feel and the obvious dedication it took to boil down a lot of research into such a small book and still make it readable are the two reasons I give this book such a high rating. Recommended."

Crowdfunding Basics In 30 Minutes

"Very understandable and absorbing. A must-read for any entrepreneur."

"On the verge of launching a crowdfunding campaign myself, this book has made me re-think my plans and my strategy. Take a step back and get the advice of someone who's been there."

LinkedIn In 30 Minutes

"This was an excellent primer for someone like me who had a LinkedIn account but didn't really use it except to look up people."

"Since reading this a week ago, I have had more quality business interactions on LinkedIn than I have had in the last 2 years."

Excel Basics In 30 Minutes

"Fast and easy. The material presented is very basic but it is also accessible with step-by-step screenshots and a friendly tone more like a friend or co-worker explaining how to use Excel than a technical manual."

"An excellent little guide. For those who already know their way around Excel, it'll be a good refresher course. Definitely plan on passing it around the office."

Twitter

In 30 Minutes

How to connect with interesting people, write great tweets, and find information that's relevant to you

THIRD EDITION

Ian Lamont

In 30 Minutes® Guides
QUICK GUIDES FOR A COMPLEX WORLD®
in30minutes.com

Twitter In 30 Minutes
Third Edition
ISBN: 978-1-64188-009-1
Library of Congress Control Number: 2015953949
Copyright © 2016-2018 by i30 Media Corporation.

Cover and interior design *by* Monica Thomas for TLC Graphics, www.TLCGraphics.com. Interior design and composition assisted *by* Rick Soldin, book-comp.com.

Printed in the United States of America.

Contents

Contents

Contents

Introduction

One January afternoon, I saw a remarkable event unfold on Twitter.

It was around 3:30 p.m., and I was sitting at my desk. A few people I followed on Twitter suddenly began sending out short text messages (called tweets) about a plane crash. The plane had apparently gone down in New York City, right in the Hudson River. New Yorkers in nearby buildings had seen the crash, or spotted a plane floating in the river, and were sharing scraps of information in the short messages that Twitter allows.

I checked CNN and Google News. There were no official news reports. Yet people on the ground were reporting a disaster. What was going on?

Then I saw someone share the following photograph on Twitter:

The fuzzy photo showed survivors standing on the wing, or stepping into a boat. The tweet that accompanied the photo said:

> *There's a plane in the Hudson. I'm on the ferry going to pick up the people. Crazy.*

I did not know Janis Krums, the person who took the photo from a passing ferry. But the photo and short message he posted on Twitter indicated that many passengers were alive, and were in the process of being rescued. Krums' friends and followers shared the message, which was shared again with thousands of other people. Considering there was no official report or news account of what was happening, it was reassuring to see Krums' tweet.

The story of US Airways Flight 1549 is now well known, thanks to the quick thinking and professionalism of Capt. Chesley B. "Sully" Sullenberger and his crew. More than 150 people were on the plane when it ran into a flock of geese and made an emergency water landing on the Hudson River. It could have been a tragedy. Yet every passenger survived.

But the incident was important for another reason: It showed that Twitter is more than just a collection of fleeting observations about everyday life. Twitter can connect people to events, information, and each other in ways that have never been experienced before.

What is Twitter?

Twitter is a free tool that can connect you with interesting people, events, and information. Twitter is available online at *twitter.com*, or as a free app that can be installed on a mobile phone or tablet. Millions of people all over the world consider Twitter to be as important to their daily communications routines as checking their email, sending text messages, or catching up with friends on Facebook.

How do people use Twitter? Here are some examples:

➤ **Abby** (@AbbyLeighTaylor) is an Oklahoma native now living in Nashville. She loves using Twitter to connect with people who share her interests in music and Mexican food.

➤ **The New York Public Library** (@nypl) tweets about library programs, author appearances, photographs from its archives, and even job openings.

➤ **Steven** (@IamStevenT) is none other than Steven Tyler, the hard-rock singer and TV personality. On Twitter, he talks about his tour schedule and television appearances, and also uses Twitter to connect with fans.

➤ **Jim A.** (@KirkLOB) is a dedicated Cleveland sports fan. Jim will respectfully debate "anything in sports," but especially likes to talk about Cleveland's professional basketball, baseball, and football teams.

➤ **Fiona** (@EmeraldFaerie), a jewelry and lighting designer based in London, uses Twitter to show off her latest creations, and let customers know where they can be purchased.

➤ **Mark** (@mcuban) is a famous entrepreneur who uses Twitter to promote his business interests and basketball team, the Dallas Mavericks. He also answers questions from fans and offers support to people who have seen him on TV or have read his book or blog.

➤ **Sockamillion** (@sockington) is Jason Scott's cat. Like many parody accounts on Twitter, the focus is on humor ("GETTING MY NAILS DONE fine just clawing the couch …"). Many of Socks' followers are pet owners who have created Twitter accounts for their cats.

Sockamillion @sockington · Jun 29
TIME TO TEACH BASIC CAT repeat after me MEOW MEOW everybody MEOW MEOW means give me food IT ALWAYS MEANS GIVE ME FOOD class dismissed MEOW

💬 2   🔁 41   ♡ 184

Sockamillion @sockington · Jun 24
COULD IT BE yes it could SOMEONE LEFT THE BASEMENT DOOR OPEN time once again for basement safari DOWN I GO step by step INTO THE DARKNESS

💬   🔁 22   ♡ 165

Sockamillion @sockington · Jun 17
HARK WHAT IS THIS THAT TICKLES MINE NOSE it appears someone is grilling ten miles away HOW DARE YOU GOOD SIR fealty is demanded HUZZAH

💬 2   🔁 12   ♡ 110

As you can see from these examples, there are all kinds of people, organizations, and interests represented on Twitter. Further, they use Twitter for varied purposes—connecting with like-minded people, promoting their businesses or causes, and having fun.

However, Twitter can be bewildering to newbies. The messages are short. There are strange symbols and unfamiliar conventions. It may not be apparent how Twitter can help you connect with people or start conversations.

The third edition of this guide is intended to help you get your bearings and teach you how to get the most out of Twitter. *Twitter In 30 Minutes* concentrates on core skills and use cases that a beginner should understand. In the next 30 minutes, you'll learn how to do everything from setting up and personalizing your account online or using a mobile phone (Chapter 2), to finding interesting people to follow (Chapter 3). There's a chapter that discusses how to tweet (Chapter 4). You'll even learn a few tricks, ranging from hashtags to retweeting (Chapter 5).

What can Twitter do for you?

At its heart, Twitter lets you do three things:

1. **Broadcast to the world what you are doing, what you are thinking, and who you are with.** The broadcasts are short messages called tweets that contain no more than 280 characters of text. It's also possible to add a photo or a link to a news story. While anyone can see these tweets, the messages are most likely to be noticed by people who *follow* you on Twitter.

2. **Monitor what other people are saying and doing, and interact with them.** Millions of ordinary people—as well as companies, schools, sports teams, charities, politicians, and superstars—broadcast their own messages to the world. You can choose to follow the accounts of people you like or who you think are interesting. When you follow someone, you will be able to see his or her recent tweets. Some may even follow you back, to see what you have to say, or start conversations with you!

3. **Learn about the world.** Because people all over the world use Twitter to describe what they are doing, how they are feeling, and what they are seeing, Twitter is a window into events, opinions, and information. Want to know what other people think about the latest episode of your favorite TV show or sports team? Want to see photographs taken at a concert, beach, or political rally? Twitter can let you do that. The flow of information is sometimes rough, but it grants an unfiltered view of the world, often before "official" sources weigh in.

In the following chapters, you'll learn how to follow people, write tweets, and engage in other activities. We only have 30 minutes, so let's get started!

CHAPTER 1

A brief tour of Twitter

Before I show you how to sign up for Twitter and start using the service, let's take a brief tour of Twitter to better understand how people use it. We'll start with a famous person (Oprah Winfrey), move onto a Twitter account operated by a local business, and then see how ordinary people use Twitter.

@Oprah

If you are sitting near a computer, or have a mobile phone, open a Web browser and type *twitter.com/oprah* into the address bar. This is the Web address for the Twitter account belonging to Oprah Winfrey, the talented American television host, actress, and media mogul. If you are sitting at a desktop computer, you will see something like this:

There's a lot going on. Photos and seemingly random messages litter the page. Elsewhere there are references to *Tweets*, *Followers*, and *Following*, along with numbers. There are buttons and strange symbols. What's happening here?

Think of *twitter.com/oprah* as Oprah's public display case. She (and her staff) determine nearly everything seen on this page. Most of the action takes place in the center of the screen. On the left side of the page, you can see Oprah's name and her Twitter name, or *handle*: @Oprah (pronounced "at-Oprah").

The front page of the @Oprah Twitter account also includes photos of Oprah, which often come from her magazine. She regularly changes the profile picture, and sometimes uses funny or striking images.

Below this are some numbers corresponding to tweets, following, and followers. Here's what the numbers mean:

➤ **Tweets**: A tweet is a message that is no more than 280 characters in length (or 140 characters in certain languages, such as Chinese and Japanese). Oprah has sent out thousands of tweets ("K" stands for "thousand"). This seems like a lot. However, she has been using Twitter for years. Considering each message takes less than a minute to compose, it's not hard to create more than one thousand tweets in a single year. Oprah's most recent tweets are shown at the top of the page. If you keep scrolling down, Oprah's older tweets will be revealed.

➤ **Following**: This number refers to other Twitter accounts that Oprah follows. There are relatively few people on the list. If you click on the number, you will see who they are. Most are media personalities, guests who have appeared on her show, and her staff. When one of them tweets something, Oprah will see it when she visits *twitter.com* or opens the Twitter app on her phone.

➤ **Followers**: Oprah has lots of fans. The "M" next to the number stands for "million." In other words, tens of millions of accounts have chosen to "follow" Oprah on Twitter. This means the people who operate the accounts will see Oprah's tweets when they look at Twitter, along with any other accounts they are following. Following a Twitter account is kind of like "friending" someone on Facebook, except it's only one-way. In other words, you can follow people on Twitter, but unlike Facebook, they don't have to follow you back. In Oprah's case, millions of people are following her, but she doesn't have to reciprocate.

Below this info are Oprah's most recent tweets. What is she talking about? Let's take a look at a sample:

It may seem jarring to see these tiny fragments of unrelated conversations on someone's Twitter profile. That's just the nature of Twitter. Later, we'll learn how to expand these conversations and even join them.

What can Oprah's tweets tell us about her interests and activities? First, she frequently engages with the people, companies, and organizations she supports, such as the National Museum of African American History and Culture (@NMAAHC).

Second, Oprah uses Twitter to promote her entertainment empire. Because she has so many followers on Twitter, mentioning or endorsing something is an extremely powerful promotional tool. Sometimes these products or ideas are associated with *hashtags*, which are words or phrases preceded by the pound symbol. In Chapter 5, we will learn more about hashtags. In Oprah's tweets, hashtags are often specific to Oprah's businesses, programs, and partnerships. For example, *#GimmeSugar* references a popular program on Oprah's cable television channel. Ralph Angel is one of the stars on the program.

Third, Oprah often discusses what she is watching on TV. It might be one of the programs on her cable channel, an awards ceremony, or a sporting event. These random snippets of text may seem strange unless you are also watching the same program at the same time. If you do happen to be watching the same program, then Oprah's comments will make perfect sense!

In terms of Oprah's popularity on Twitter, it should be noted that the @Oprah account is unusual. Oprah was famous *before* she joined Twitter, and has her own television network, which explains her army of followers.

This is rare. Very few people and organizations have this level of influence on Twitter. It's far more common to have just a few hundred followers. As you might expect, having a few hundred followers vs. millions of followers changes the nature of the discussions and interactions on Twitter.

@Momogoose

For our second example, we're going to look at a local business. Momogoose operates food trucks and the Sate Grill in the Boston area. I discovered the food trucks when I was a graduate student, and was surprised to see that they had a Twitter handle—@momogoose—painted on the exterior of the trucks. What could a food truck possibly have to say on Twitter? A lot, it turns out. Here's *twitter.com/momogoose:*

Like Oprah, Momogoose uses Twitter for promotional purposes and reaching out to fans. But the scale is much smaller. Momogoose only has a few thousand followers, and most of them are in the Boston area.

Why do these people follow a food truck on Twitter? Obviously, they like the trucks and the food, and following @momogoose on Twitter is a way of showing support. But it's also a way of finding out about Momogoose, the business.

Indeed, @momogoose sends out a regular stream of tweets on weekdays describing new dishes or specials. Based on these tweets, some followers may decide to visit one of the trucks. Even if the result is only two or three additional sales per day, that adds up over time. For Momogoose, Twitter is a free promotional tool that can help attract customers and generate revenue.

Momogoose also uses Twitter to connect with customers and other businesses in other ways. Some Twitter users ask questions, while others give feedback. @Momogoose is only too happy to engage with its customers using Twitter. Momogoose also follows many of its fans, as well as other local businesses.

@RobertFischer

Robert Fischer may not be a celebrity, but he is a very active person on Twitter, with tens of thousands of tweets. Here is his profile, located at *twitter. com/RobertFischer:*

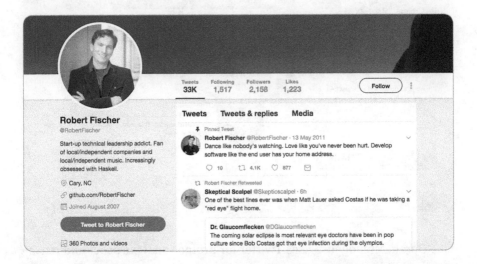

@RobertFischer puts his interests front and center for other people to see. This helps potential followers decide whether or not to follow him.

The topics @RobertFischer tweets about run the gamut from bluegrass to programming to politics. Every now and then, he'll throw out a link to a funny video. He is very engaged with the people he follows and his followers—he frequently responds to questions or comments on Twitter, and also uses it to ask questions related to software development and other topics.

@Jus_Tish

Like @RobertFisher, @Jus_Tish is a normal person (as opposed to a celebrity) using Twitter to talk about her interests and reach out to friends. Here's her profile page at *twitter.com/jus_tish:*

One thing that's worth noting: The identity of @Jus_Tish is not entirely clear. While she has a profile photo, she chose to use a nickname for her Twitter handle, and does not reveal any information about her hometown or occupation. Twitter asks all new users to enter a full name when they register, but it's also possible to use nicknames, initials, and fanciful identities. Anonymous or semi-anonymous Twitter identities give people more flexibility in terms of what they say and how they present themselves.

What does @Jus_Tish tweet about? She loves going to church. She likes music—about half of her tweets relate to something she's listening to or watching on YouTube. She actively participates in discussions about one of her favorite singers, Calvin Richardson (@IamCalvin). She likes Chinese food, and sometimes tweets about what she is watching on TV. @Jus_Tish also reaches out to a small circle of Twitter connections to offer reassurance, updates, or observations about life. Her tweets are sprinkled with quotes.

@Jus_Tish tweets a lot. On some days, Tish sends dozens of tweets. How can she do it? She uses the mobile Twitter app. This allows her to tweet from practically anywhere.

@Caliguy16

There is one last Twitter account I want to use as an example. Here's the account for @caliguy16:

As you start to use Twitter, you will see many accounts that have an image of a silhouette instead of a person or logo. Why use a silhouette? If someone starts an account but doesn't provide a profile picture, then Twitter will default to a graphic of a silhouette on a colored background. The different colors don't mean anything, but the silhouette is associated with "newbie" accounts, belonging to people who just got started with Twitter or those who abandoned the accounts not long after registering them. Indeed, @ caliguy16 tweeted many years ago and then quit Twitter.

It's not clear why @caliguy16 gave up. If I were to hazard a guess, I would point to the lack of a network. He never followed anyone and was followed by only one person—a local politician who barely used Twitter himself. Because @caliguy16 did not follow anyone, this means there would have been no information or people to talk with in his timeline. If you don't build your network, Twitter will seem like a lonely and boring place.

I also want to mention something about the silhouette icon. While there's nothing wrong with being a newbie on Twitter, there's no excuse for not replacing the silhouette with a real image. Silhouette profiles send negative signals to other people on Twitter, who may avoid following accounts that do not appear very dedicated to the Twitter community.

Fortunately, it's easy enough to create and upload a profile picture using your phone or *twitter.com*. I'll show you how to do this in the next chapter.

CHAPTER 2

Signing up for Twitter

There are two ways to sign up for Twitter: online (using a Web browser on your PC or laptop), or on a mobile device (such as a phone or tablet). Both ways are easy. I recommend registering online, using a desktop or laptop computer, because you are less likely to make a typing mistake (important for usernames and passwords).

If you already have a Twitter account, you can skip the registration steps. However, you may still be interested in the sections that describe the Twitter interface (including the icons) and customization options.

How to register online

Open up your Web browser, and type *twitter.com* into the address bar. You should see something like this:

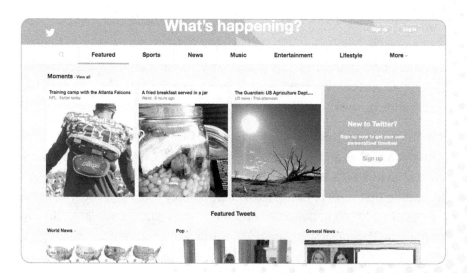

Scroll down to the *Sign up* button to be brought to the registration screen. To create a Twitter account, you have to supply a name. It can be your full name, your first name, your initials, the name of a business, or an alias. You also need to submit an identifier such as a phone number or valid email address. Twitter uses this information to confirm the account and send you notifications.

Leave the *Personalize Twitter* checkbox unchecked. If you select this option, Twitter will track your browsing history on sites that contain Twitter widgets and display advertisements, recommendations, and other content based on what you've viewed on other websites. Imagine what sorts of assumptions Twitter will make based on the sites your 7-year-old son checks out, or the fact that you once looked up the Home Depot website to see what time the nearest branch closes. Twitter may assume you love Legos and riding mowers, and will mercilessly bombard you with such ads. My advice: Leave this box unchecked.

Twitter will send a verification code to your email or phone number. Enter the code into the space provided, and click *Verify*. Create a password, and enter the other information as prompted. Certain screens can be skipped. For instance, if you register with your phone number and you don't want to enter your email address, click the *Skip* link when prompted.

Pick a suitable Twitter handle

One thing you should not skip is choosing a username. Whatever letters, numbers, and characters you choose will become your Twitter handle. Twitter suggests usernames based on the name used at the beginning of the registration process:

But there's a problem. Twitter has suggested I choose something like "IanIanlamont" as a username. I don't want to have @IanIanlamont as my Twitter handle—it's strange, long, and hard for others to remember. I want something that is more personal or relates to my company. The username "ian" is already taken, but the username "author_ianl" is available. So, my Twitter handle will be @author_ianl.

Choose a username.

Don't worry, you can always change it later.

| ianlamont | ✕ This username is already taken! |

Suggestions: Ianlanlamont | Ianlamontian | Ianlamontinfo | Infolanlamont | Ian_Ianlamont

Next

Skip

Some people like to use Twitter usernames that are similar to their real names. For instance, the singer Alicia Keys uses @aliciakeys. My personal Twitter account, which I have used since 2007, is @ilamont. The official Twitter handle for IN 30 MINUTES guides is @in30minutes. Handles like this are easy to remember, but some people don't want to directly connect their identities to Twitter. What's more, it's difficult to choose handles based on common names, because other people may have already chosen them.

Twitter allows people to change usernames, but I advise picking a username you like and sticking with it. Here are some additional things to keep in mind when it comes to picking a good Twitter username/handle:

➤ Avoid long usernames, which are usually difficult to remember.

➤ Usernames that are similar to other well-known accounts may lead to confusion.

➤ Usernames that harass or ridicule ("@cats_are_evil") may limit your ability to make connections or could lead to angry conversations.

How Twitter uses topics to recommend accounts

Twitter is a social network. Not only can you create 280-character tweets and post photos, you are also supposed to follow other people—friends, strangers, celebrities, businesses, and even @sockington the cat. Following their Twitter accounts lets you see the tweets that they create, which shows their interests and daily lives.

Twitter wants you to start following people right away. After choosing a username, Twitter suggests certain accounts based on the topics that interest you. Choices include:

➤ Sports

➤ Music

➤ Photography

➤ Entertainment

➤ Fun

➤ News

➤ Technology

➤ Government & Politics

Select the topics that interest you, and proceed to the next screen.

Upload contact lists to Twitter

Twitter can help you find friends to follow by looking at the email addresses and phone numbers in your Yahoo, Gmail, or other contact lists. Twitter will match the contact data in your address book with existing Twitter accounts, which are then recommended to you.

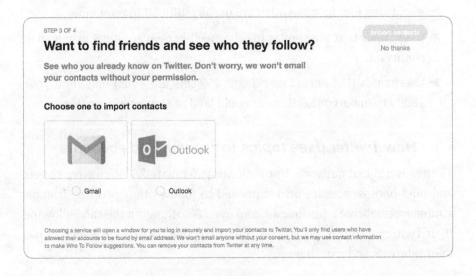

I have mixed feelings about this service. It's a very convenient way to find friends and colleagues with Twitter accounts, even if they are using an obscure Twitter handle.

However, there are pitfalls associated with letting Twitter gather all the email addresses in your address book:

➤ Twitter may ask for your consent to spam your own contact list with Twitter invitations.

➤ Twitter may use the data for other purposes, from building profiles of new users based on their address book connections to targeting people with certain types of advertisements.

It's spammy, and you have little control over how Twitter uses the data. I recommend clicking the *No thanks* link.

Recommended accounts to follow

Next, you will be shown a list of recommended Twitter accounts to follow. Twitter's recommendations are mostly popular accounts with lots of followers. You will have a chance to follow ordinary folks later. Select the ones you like, or batch-follow all of them.

Before you continue, you may be prompted to turn on browser notifications. If you agree, your browser will display tweets and other notifications in the browser even if you are not on Twitter. It's a major distraction if you are using the browser for email or something else. I recommend skipping this option.

Begin using Twitter

At this point, you will be brought to your home timeline. You may see some tips about how to use the timeline and other features:

To say hello, click on the field that says, "What's happening?" and type a short greeting. Suggestions for making great tweets can be found in Chapter 4.

How to register using a phone or tablet

Registering on a mobile phone or tablet is quick. You will need to download the Twitter mobile app first, though. Twitter makes apps for most mobile platforms, including:

➤ **Android**: Phones and tablets from Samsung, Xiaomi, Nexus, and many others.

➤ **iOS**: The iPhone, iPad, and iPod touch

➤ **BlackBerry phones**

➤ **Windows phones and tablets**

➤ **Other devices** such as the Apple Watch

In this section, I'll cover Android and iOS devices, which dominate the market. The Twitter app can be downloaded via Apple's App Store and Google Play. Setup processes are nearly identical. If you have a Windows Phone, BlackBerry, or another device, go to *twitter.com/download* to get the app.

How to install Twitter on an iPhone or iPad

The Twitter apps for the iPhone and iPad look great, and generally perform very well, thanks to the standard iOS interfaces and powerful Apple hardware.

Registering for Twitter on your iPhone or iPad is easy:

1. Open the Apple App Store, and download the Twitter app.

2. Once installed, press the *Sign up* button (press the *Log in* button if you have already created an account online).

3. On the next screen, enter your name (or initials), phone number, username, and password. (Your username must be unique to Twitter. See *Pick a suitable Twitter handle* earlier in this chapter for more information.)

4. If you want to use an email address instead of a phone number to register, tap the *Use email instead* link. *Advanced options* allow users to let friends find them by phone number or email address.

5. Press the blue button to create your account.

The app will prompt you to allow Twitter to access your phone's location data. Why? Twitter wants to "customize your experience," which includes showing local accounts—and local ads. You can also add your location to tweets, which can be fun if you want to share your photos from restaurants, trips, professional sporting events, or concerts.

The Twitter app may also ask if it can access the contact list on your iOS device. Agreeing to this will let Twitter match the email addresses in your contact list with existing Twitter accounts. Because of Twitter's spammy policies around the use of users' address books, I recommend users reject the app's requests to access this data. There will be other ways to connect with friends and interesting people, as described later in this guide.

How to install Twitter on Android

Because there are many flavors of Android, you may see some variations in the interface, depending on which flavor of Android you use.

Here's how to get started:

1. Open Google Play on your Android device (phone, tablet, etc.) and search for Twitter.

2. Tap the *Install* button.

3. Google Play will show you which features the Twitter app will be able to access. You must approve this to continue the installation process.

4. Open the app.

You will see something like this:

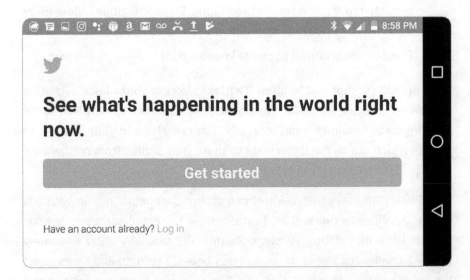

Tap the blue button to start the registration process. Tap *Log in* if you already have already created a Twitter account online or on another device.

The registration screen has fields for Name, Email, Username (which will determine your Twitter handle) and phone number. It's almost identical to the iOS version. However, the Android interface for tweeting and changing your profile is quite different.

Navigating the Twitter interface

Once you have registered for Twitter, you may wonder how to navigate the service, and how to use certain features. This section will help you get your bearings, and explain what all of the icons, links, and buttons are for.

The Twitter icons explained

Twitter.com and the Twitter mobile app use icons to perform common functions. There are slight variations between the Web, Android, and iOS versions of the icons.

On *twitter.com*, the Twitter toolbar runs across the top of the browser window:

Here is a brief description of the icons, and the functions they perform:

➤ **Home**: The icon looks like a birdhouse, and takes you to the home timeline view.

➤ **Moments**: The lightning bolt icon displays news articles, viral videos, and other content that is trending or widely discussed on Twitter.

➤ **Notifications**: Click on the bell to see recent interactions with your Twitter account, such as someone following you, mentioning your Twitter account, or retweeting one of your tweets.

➤ **Direct messages**: The icon that looks like an envelope shows a list of private messages between you and mutual followers.

➤ **Search box**: Lets you search for words or phrases mentioned on Twitter, as well as accounts belonging to specific people and organizations. On the Twitter mobile app, tap the icon that looks like a magnifying glass.

➤ **Profile icon**: Click or tap the profile icon (based on your profile photo) to adjust settings, access help resources, or log out.

➤ **Compose new tweet**: The blue button lets you write a new tweet.

The Twitter apps for Android and iOS have additional icons:

➤ **Tweet icon.** The mobile apps use a small button that looks like a quill to compose a new tweet.

➤ **Profile icon.** On iOS and Android devices, tapping your profile icon will bring up options to view your profile, switch accounts (if you have more than one Twitter account), and view Lists and Moments.

➤ **More actions.** The icon that looks like three vertical dots shows more actions, including reporting or blocking users or sharing profiles and tweets in email, messaging apps, or other social networks.

➤ **Follow.** tap the *Follow* button appearing at the top of a profile to follow that person's tweets.

There are icons associated with individual tweets, too:

➤ **Reply.** The speech-bubble icon lets you reply to a specific tweet (see Chapter 5).

➤ **Retweet.** The two circling arrows will retweet the selected tweet (see the section on *Retweets* in Chapter 5).

➤ **Like.** The heart icon will add the tweet to a personal list of likes (which can be accessed via your profile, above your personal timeline).

➤ **Analytics.** The icon that looks like a tiny bar chart shows how many other people saw the tweet or interacted with it in some way (retweet, profile view, etc.).

➤ **Drop-down options.** The downward-pointing arrow activates a menu that shows additional options for the selected tweet, including the ability to delete it.

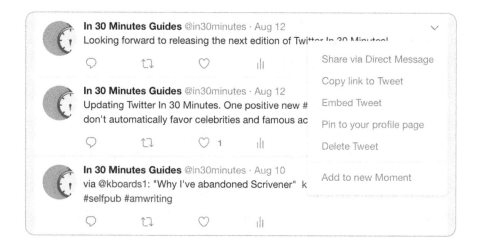

Your home timeline

The first time you log in to Twitter, you'll see a page containing your basic profile as well as a list of recent tweets created by other people you follow, as well as advertisements. Here's what it looks like for my new account:

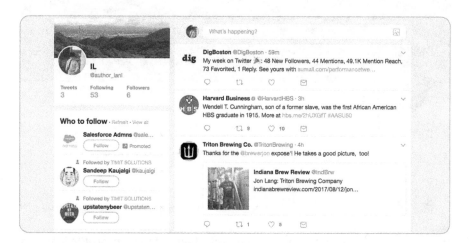

This is my *home timeline*. At this point, I follow a limited number of Twitter accounts, so there will only be a limited amount of activity. Over time, this view will change as I start to follow friends, colleagues, local people, and other accounts that interest me. In Chapter 3, I outline an approach for selecting Twitter accounts to follow, which will make for a more rewarding experience.

The first time you visit your own profile on *twitter.com*, you may also be prompted to send out one of several premade tweets. Click the Tweet icons, or write your own in the field provided.

Your personal timeline

Every Twitter account has its own timeline, which shows a list of recent tweets created by the account's owner. Earlier in this guide, we saw snapshots of the timelines belonging to @Oprah, @Momogoose, and @RobertFischer. You can see practically any timeline by clicking on that person's or organization's Twitter handle. Profile information appears first, but if you scroll down, the entire timeline will gradually become visible.

You can also view your own personal timeline. On *twitter.com*, click your profile photo or handle:

If you are using the Twitter app on a mobile device, tap your profile icon and then *Profile* to see your own timeline.

How to customize your profile

Before you start using Twitter, consider customizing your bio and adding a header photo. Personalizing your small corner of Twitter can make it more comfortable for you. It can also help attract more followers.

Edit profile information

Access your profile information by clicking or tapping your profile photo, and then selecting *Edit profile*:

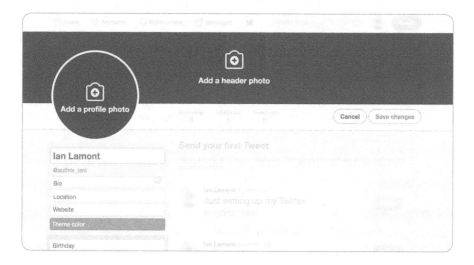

Profile information includes your *Name*, *Bio*, *Location*, and *Website*. You don't need to fill out all of the fields, but I do recommend adding a short bio. A good bio can convey your personality or interests to other Twitter users, which in turn can lead to better followers and conversations.

The bio has to be less than 160 characters. You may want to use funny descriptors ("Sharp-dressed taco aficionado and die-hard Eagles fan") or something more down-to-earth ("Real estate lawyer serving greater Phoenix"). I chose something in between, with a cute picture of myself at age 4, and a tame message about what I do and what I like ("Author of In 30 Minutes guides. Cat lover.")

Location can be a city, a country, a state, or even a state of mind—Twitter doesn't verify accuracy, so you can put whatever you are comfortable sharing. *Website* is generally a personal website, blog, or business website, but many people leave this field blank.

Next, you can customize other elements of your profile, including the header and theme color.

Add a header photo

The header photo appears above your profile photo. To add one on *twitter. com*, go to the *Edit profile* screen and follow these steps:

1. Click *Add a header photo* to browse your hard drive.

2. Twitter recommends an image that is 1500 pixels wide and 500 pixels tall. Don't worry if you don't know what a pixel is or how to get the image to fit these dimensions. Twitter will let you crop or zoom using a normal-sized digital photo.

3. After you upload the photo and apply it to your profile, click *Save changes*.

If you decide to replace the profile picture or header photo, go to the Profile settings and follow the steps listed above.

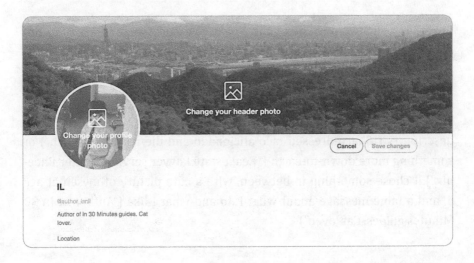

Add photos and a bio using the Twitter app

The Twitter app for phones and tablets will prompt new users to customize their profiles with photos and a brief bio. It's very convenient, as you can use selfies and other photos taken with the phone's camera. To edit your profile, follow these steps:

Android:

1. Open the Android app, and press the profile icon.

2. Tap your Twitter handle to open your profile.

3. Tap the *Edit profile* button.

iPhone or iPad:

1. Open the app, and press the profile icon.

2. Select *Profile*.

3. Tap the *Edit profile* button.

CHAPTER 3

Finding and following people on Twitter

Now that you have activated your Twitter account, you can start tweeting right away. (This is explained in more detail in the next chapter). First, however, we are going to cover the art of finding and following interesting accounts. Doing so will boost your Twitter experience in several important ways:

➤ The more people you follow, the more likely you are to see interesting things that you can share, explore, or respond to.

➤ Some people you follow on Twitter will follow you back, which can help build your Twitter network and increase the likelihood of your tweets being seen and responded to.

How to follow someone on Twitter

You've signed up for Twitter, reserved your Twitter handle, set up a profile, and are ready to seize Twitter by the beak. This requires tweeting (described in Chapter 4), but you also want to see what other people are tweeting about and sharing on Twitter.

To see other people's tweets, you'll need to start following people. If you don't, Twitter will seem empty and boring, and you will quickly lose interest.

As described earlier in this guide, Twitter encourages new users to follow celebrities, and other popular accounts. Twitter also prompts users to upload their address books, and will try to match the email addresses of friends and other contacts with existing Twitter accounts.

But what if you want to follow a Twitter account later on? The following sections explain how.

Follow an account online

Once you are registered for Twitter and have logged in, clicking on another person's Twitter handle will reveal that person's Twitter profile. Each profile contains a *Follow* button. Click it to follow the account. Once you do that, that person's tweets will start appearing in your home timeline.

Below is an example of @marty_walsh, the Twitter profile of Boston's mayor. You can visit his profile by typing *twitter.com/marty_walsh* into the address bar of your browser. The *Follow* button is located on the right side of his profile:

If you click the button, recent tweets created by Mayor Walsh (as well as tweets posted by staff on his behalf) will start to appear in your home timeline. Your home timeline consists of tweets from the Twitter accounts you follow, with Twitter's algorithm giving additional weight to accounts you regularly interact with or tweets that receive lots of retweets, comments, and likes. The more accounts you follow, the more tweets you will see in your timeline. Twitter also inserts advertisements into the timeline.

Follow an account using the Twitter app

If you are using the Twitter app on your mobile device, tapping the handle of a Twitter user will reveal his or her profile. Click the *Follow* button to start following them:

Alternately, you can use the Twitter app's search feature to find specific accounts to follow:

1. Look for an icon that looks like a magnifying glass. Tap it to open the search feature.

2. In the field provided, type the account name or the name of the person or organization you want to follow.

3. The names of likely accounts will start to automatically appear below the search field.

4. Once you have found the right account, click the *Follow* button.

Who should you follow?

Twitter has many mechanisms to help users find people to follow. If you've registered for Twitter (Chapter 2), you have noticed how Twitter suggests accounts belonging to famous people or organizations. Twitter can also leverage your address book list to identify friends and coworkers who are already on Twitter.

However, the sheer number of accounts and topics being discussed can be confusing to novice users. What's the best approach for deciding who to follow?

➤ **For a rewarding Twitter experience, it's crucial to identify accounts that are close to your own connections and interests.** They might be friends, family members, or colleagues. They could be people living in your town or city, or people from a location that's close to your heart—the place where you grew up, a favorite vacation spot, or a city or country you would like to visit.

➤ **I also advise new Twitter users to follow people who have common causes or similar hobbies.** Identify the experts or people with the best insights. Seek out sources of information that lead the conversation, such as a well-known publication, pundit, or thought leader. They don't have to be celebrities. In fact, many of the examples that follow are almost unknown outside of their areas of expertise.

Experts and leaders

Do you like political news? Are you the kind of person who feels a tingle of excitement when there's a scandal brewing, or do you like to follow wonky policy debates? Then follow @Politico, which is the Twitter account for the popular Washington-based news site of the same name. Political junkies may also want to follow the accounts of certain reporters, pundits, politicians, and government officials.

Maybe you are a knitting fanatic. If that's the case, then @KnittingDaily is a good account to follow. People in this community share tips and new designs. There are even indie knitting rebels at @YarnHarlot.

Basketball freaks have their own Twitter buzz. This is due in large part to the active participation by professional and college players, as well as their fans. I recommend @SLAMonline or @ESPNNBA, as well as the accounts of individual players.

The disability community has developed a strident voice on Twitter. People with spinal cord injuries, low-vision users, and patients with other health conditions share their views of the world. There are advocacy efforts promoted by disability rights activists and family members. The accounts operated by Paralympic gold medalist @JessicaLong and @AAPD are good places to start.

At the start of this guide, I described the account of @sockington the cat. **What if you're a dog person?** Twitter has you covered! A popular Twitter dog is @JamesBondTheDog ("international hound dog of mystery"), with thousands of followers on Twitter.

You get the idea. **Practically every interest, hobby, cause, and condition is represented on Twitter.** Sometimes it takes a little digging to find relevant and interesting accounts (more on that below), but once you follow them, you will feel connected to a group of kindred souls (or cats).

How to find specific accounts to follow

So you have an idea of who you want to follow. The next step is actually locating the accounts on Twitter.

It's not as easy as it sounds. While some people have obvious account names (such as @Oprah) others choose unusual Twitter handles. For instance, actor Ashton Kutcher uses @aplusk.

While many ordinary people use handles based on their actual names, it may not be clear which account should be followed if there are other Twitter users with similar names and handles.

However, there are ways of cutting through the confusion.

Twitter search

Twitter's search engine is a useful way to find accounts to follow. On the Twitter mobile app, tap the magnifying glass to open the search window. On *twitter.com*, the search window is located at the top of the page. Just start typing in names, and people's accounts will automatically begin to show up below the field:

Press *Enter* on your keyboard to show a list of results, which can be narrowed down further by selecting *People*.

This is a great way to find specific people. I've been able to track down the Twitter accounts of musicians, businesspeople, authors, and old friends in this manner. However, Twitter search has limitations:

➤ Some people use Twitter without revealing their real names in their profiles. If you search for their names, you may not be able to find them.

➤ People with common names can be difficult to find on Twitter—there may be scores or hundreds of people with the same name who show up in search results.

Here's an example that helps illustrate the problem. Let's say I wanted to find Bill Lee, the quirky Red Sox pitching ace from the 1970s known as "Spaceman" to his many fans. Typing "Bill Lee" into Twitter's search engine brings back a list of other men and women named Bill Lee, William Lee, or Billie Lee, but not my childhood baseball hero. However, by changing the search terms to "Spaceman Bill Lee," he shows up:

Another method involves searching for words or phrases. Let's say you wanted to find other people who like Oprah's Book Club. Searching for that phrase brings up some interesting results, ranging from a link to the official Oprah's Book Club account on Twitter to random tweets by readers:

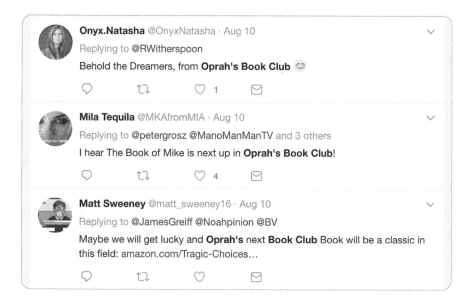

You can use the same technique to search for local accounts. For instance, if you like Chicago basketball, search for "Chicago Bulls" or the name of a Bulls player. If you are interested in politics in San Diego, search for "San Diego politics" or the name of the mayor.

After pressing *Enter* on your keyboard, Twitter shows what it thinks are the most relevant results under the *Top* tab. Top accounts and top tweets have either been created by people with an extensive Twitter presence, or the tweets have been widely shared on Twitter. Be sure to click the *Latest* tab to see the posts by everyone else, which may be more interesting or detailed than the Top tweets. *People* shows Twitter accounts belonging to people, organizations, or causes, while *Photos* and *Videos* shows media content that people have uploaded to Twitter. *News* and *Broadcast* displays news and video associated with the search terms.

Find friends on Twitter

Twitter is used by hundreds of millions of people, so there is a good chance that at least a few people you know have active Twitter accounts. You may have encountered them when you registered your account, if you used the option that lets Twitter scan your contact lists.

There are other ways to find friends on Twitter. In addition to Twitter's search engine, The easiest way to do it is to ask ... on Facebook! Here's what you can post on Facebook:

> *"Friends, I am building up my Twitter network at @bobsmith102. Please follow me or your leave your Twitter handle in the comments to this post."*

The same technique can be used on LinkedIn, Instagram, or other social networks and messaging services.

You can also search for people's Twitter handles on Google, Bing, or other search engines. Just type a name and "twitter" and see what turns up. Note, however, that this method will not identify people who used their real names when they registered for Twitter.

How to find local accounts

The great thing about tapping into local accounts in Twitter is that it allows you to gain new insights into your community and the people who live there.

Here are common starting points:

Local media: You may already get the local paper delivered to your house, or tune into the local TV news from time to time. I have found that Twitter accounts operated by local media sometimes have extra goodies, including live reports from local events or details that get left out of the 10 o'clock news. To start following a media account, you'll have to find the Twitter profile first. If it can't be found in Twitter's search engine, go to the online presence of the news organization. The home page will often have a little blurb that says "Follow us on Twitter!" with either a link to the Twitter profile or the account name preceded by the @ symbol.

For instance, my local paper's Twitter account is @NewtonTab. To go to the Twitter profile, I just type *twitter.com/newtontab* in the address bar of the browser.

Besides links to online news stories or breaking police and fire incidents, additional information gets shared. Here's one update from my local paper, talking about a local baseball game:

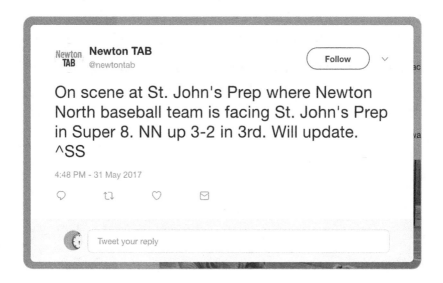

The reporter who wrote it let followers know that updates would be provided throughout the game. He also shared the location, in case residents wanted to watch in person. This is information local people can use!

Besides following the account of the paper or individual reporters, you can also use local media accounts to find other local people or institutions to follow. For instance, local news outlets in Boston often retweet messages from Boston's mayor, Marty Walsh (@marty_walsh).

From the profile, all I need to do is press the *Follow* button, and I'll be able to see the mayor's tweets in my timeline.

Local bloggers: Somewhere in your community, someone is writing a blog. Blog authors are people who feel compelled to write about topics that are important to them. It could be about their lives, their hobbies or interests, their children, their areas of expertise, or even uncomfortable topics such as living with disease or divorce.

You may not know who these people are. Indeed, they may not want you to know who they are, but they are there, and they love to write. They often love to tweet, too.

To find local bloggers who write about local issues, Google "blog" and the name of your town or community. Check out the blogs that are highlighted, and look for a Twitter symbol on the front page. Click the symbol to be taken to the blogger's Twitter account. If you like what you see, follow the account!

For instance, one of the top results for "Boston blog" is Universal Hub. The site has an active Twitter account at @UniversalHub:

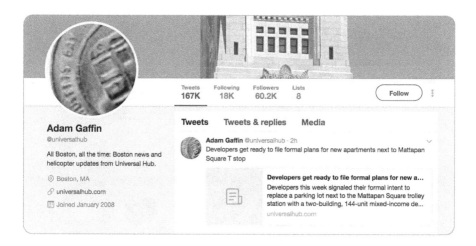

Local businesses and organizations: In Chapter 1, I used the example of the @momogoose food truck, which uses Twitter to stay connected with its customers. Many other local businesses also use Twitter. The next time you visit a local coffee shop, clothes boutique, restaurant, or library, look around for a "Follow us on Twitter!" sign. These days, savvy businesses use Twitter to connect with local patrons who want to learn about incoming products, special deals, new branches, or other insights.

You don't need to visit the building in person to find out if a business has a Twitter account. Google the company online, and see if the company's website contains a link to a Twitter account.

Random local people: Once you've identified local media, bloggers, and businesses, and are following them on Twitter, check out the *Following* and *Followers* links on their profile pages. You're sure to find local people in the lists. For instance, in @UniversalHub's list of followers, I found these Twitter accounts:

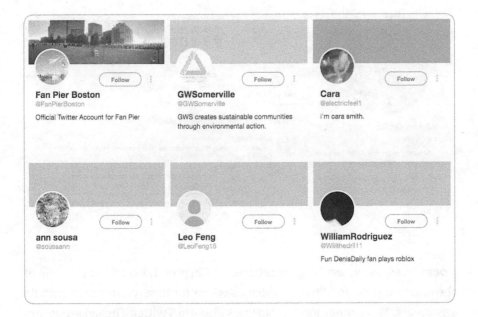

Clicking through to the profiles, I was able to identify lots of people living in the Boston area. How? Sometimes people include their hometowns on their Twitter profiles, or they may reference people, places, or issues in their tweets that give clues to where they are located.

You can do the same thing, starting with local media and businesses and trying to identify local followers. You may not know these people, and they may not use their real names on Twitter. Nevertheless, it's OK to follow them. They may even follow you back!

Twitter's recommendation algorithm

If you are using Twitter on the Web, you'll notice a list of recommended accounts when you go to your home page at *twitter.com*. They are listed under the *Who to follow* box:

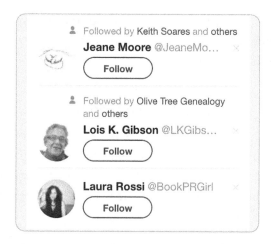

Twitter uses algorithms and behavioral data to generate the recommendations. So, if you follow sports teams and athletes, you can expect to see similar accounts in the *Who to follow* box. From time to time, interesting accounts will show up, and they can be immediately followed. Click the "X" to dismiss a recommended account. Click *View all* to see a long list of recommendations.

If you're a new user, there may not be enough behavioral data to generate recommendations. As a result, the *Who to follow* box is more likely to show famous people, news services, and promoted accounts (products, brands, and other accounts that pay Twitter to be featured recommendations).

How many accounts should a new user follow?

How many people and organizations should you follow on Twitter? That's up to you. I have seen people who follow tens of thousands of other Twitter accounts. While they never have a shortage of tweets to read, I question the value of the information they are getting in their home timelines—the most interesting or relevant information tends to be lost in the fire hose of tweets.

A better strategy, at least in the beginning, is to follow a limited number of people or organizations that are more likely to maintain your interest and engage with you. Once you've gotten the hang of Twitter, grow the list as slowly or as quickly as you like.

Following 100 other Twitter accounts is a good starting point. It doesn't take that long to follow 100 accounts, and if you pick wisely, you'll start getting value from your list right away.

Protected accounts

A small number of Twitter accounts are partially closed off to public view. The profile picture, total numbers of followers, and other information are shown. However, the owner's tweets, the identities of followers, and the accounts he or she is following are hidden. A small lock icon on the profile indicates that the account is *protected*.

Why would someone set up a protected Twitter account, or switch his or her account from open to protected status? Here are some reasons:

➤ The owner does not want to share his or her tweets for personal reasons, or because of a desire for privacy.

➤ Certain people, such as a celebrity embroiled in a scandal, may want to temporarily avoid scrutiny. He or she will re-open the account once the hubbub dies down.

➤ People or organizations want to reserve a Twitter handle so no one else grabs it, but the owner is not ready to start tweeting.

It is possible to follow a protected account. However, you will first need to be approved by the owner. Simply click the *Follow* button, and a notification will be sent to the owner of the account. He or she can then approve or reject the request. If you are approved, you will be able to see the account's personal timeline.

If you get rejected, don't take it hard. There are many other interesting accounts to follow, as we will see later this chapter.

Accounts to avoid

Before I follow accounts, I check their tweets. If a certain account rarely tweets, or the tweets are boring (for instance, just links to news stories) I won't follow the account. Here are some other red flags:

Silhouette accounts. Silhouette accounts are often new or abandoned accounts, created by people who haven't uploaded a profile picture to Twitter. For people who have just started tweeting, a silhouette account is normal. (Maybe you're a silhouette, too!) However, silhouette accounts that haven't been updated in months or years are not worth following. The people who own them have given up on Twitter, and most likely won't ever share something of interest.

Rude birds. Some people on Twitter use Twitter to belittle others, spread bizarre observations, or share intimate details of their warped lives. The tweets are littered with swears and stupidity. Sometimes the accounts belong to teens who don't know any better. Sometimes they belong to adults who haven't matured. Rarely do they offer insights or information of value. Don't bother following them.

Spam accounts. Not long after you start using Twitter, you will receive a notification that someone is following you. Most of the time, the followers are legitimate—maybe they are people you know, or people who are following you because of some shared interest.

But others may look a little … off. The tweets seem vapid or inauthentic. They follow hundreds or thousands of people, but have very few people following them back. Links appear in their feeds that don't come from well-known domains. In addition, the profile pictures tend to show unusually attractive people. Here's an example:

Don't get your hopes up if someone like this follows you. Random attractive people probably don't want to follow you (or me, for that matter). In fact, such accounts do not belong to attractive strangers tweeting about football, travel, and hooking up. These accounts actually belong to spammers, and my guess is most of them are unattractive, basement-dwelling losers who tweet links to low-grade dating sites, advertisements, or online shopping portals that might generate a few pennies every time someone clicks. Don't click the links, and don't follow them back!

How to unfollow a Twitter account

Here's the situation: You're following a famous athlete, but the relentless promotion of his corporate sponsors is driving you nuts. It's gotten to the point that when his profile picture pops up in your Twitter feed, you involuntarily groan in anticipation of another plug of his favorite sports drink, athletic shoe, or breakfast cereal. Please, make it stop!

The easy way to unfollow anyone on Twitter is to simply click the *Unfollow* button on his or her profile. For instance, to unfollow the athlete on the Twitter website, you would go to his online Twitter profile. The *Following* button confirms you are following him, but if you hover your mouse over the button, it turns into an *Unfollow* button:

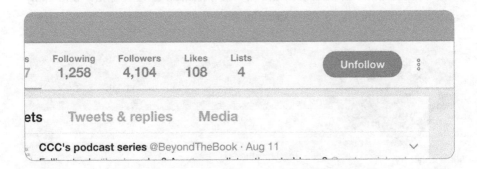

Once you have unfollowed the athlete, his tweets will no longer be automatically fed into your home timeline. Huzzah!

How to mute accounts

There is another way to silence a person's account without unfollowing him or her. Here's how to do it:

1. Go to *twitter.com* and click the *Followers* link.

2. The page will display a list of accounts following you. Find the account you want to mute.

3. Next to the *Follow* button is the More Actions icon (three dots). Click it, and select *Mute*.

The person will still think you are a follower, but you won't see his or her tweets unless he or she replies to one of your tweets, or mentions you.

How to quickly unfollow lots of people

If you want to unfollow lots of people at once, there is an easy way to do it. Go to your own profile and select *Following*. Doing so brings up a list of all of the Twitter accounts you are following. Hover over one of the *Follow* buttons to show the unfollow option, and click. Repeat for any other accounts that no longer interest you.

On the mobile app, here are the steps to unfollow accounts:

1. Open the Twitter app, and go to your own Twitter profile.

2. Press *Following*.

3. You will see a list of accounts that you are currently following, with a small *Following* button next to each profile. Press the button next to each account you want to unfollow.

Help! I'm being followed

What happens when someone follows you on Twitter? You may see a message like this in your email inbox:

You can also see a list of all of your followers. Go to your profile page on Twitter and click the *Followers* link. All of the accounts following you will be presented in reverse-chronological order.

It may seem strange that these people are following your tweets. Who are they? How did they find out about you? What are their intentions?

For most accounts, it is easy to figure out who they are: Just click on the link to see their profile page and the recent tweets they've made.

As for how they found out about you, and why they are following you, those are harder questions to answer. In many cases, they may have stumbled upon you by using Twitter's search engine or looking at someone else's list of followers (for instance, if you follow @Oprah or the local newspaper, you will show up on those two accounts' lists of followers). They may think your tweets are funny or insightful, or you share some common interest.

Most of the time, it's harmless attention. These strangers will see your tweets, and may even start a dialogue at some point.

But "following" is not synonymous with "stalking." Twitter creates value by sharing information and letting people and organizations expand their networks, even with strangers who they may never meet in person.

Remember also that anyone can see your tweets. All they need to do is load your profile into their Web browsers. Even if they aren't following you, they will still see your tweets.

In other words, your tweets are public. If you don't want anyone to see them, then you should protect your tweets … or not use Twitter at all.

Information on how to block specific users from following you and how to protect your tweets is described below.

How to block followers

Twitter says it is committed to cracking down on abuse, including online harassment. If someone starts following you and you don't want them to, you can block them. You can also report them, which notifies Twitter they may be harassing you or engaging in behavior that Twitter prohibits. Here's how to block or report an account online:

1. Go to *twitter.com* and click the *Followers* link.
2. The page will display a list of accounts following you. Find the account you want to block.
3. Next to the *Follow* button is the More Actions icon (three dots). Click it, and select *Block* or *Report*.

If you are using the Twitter mobile app, follow these steps to block another user:

1. Open the app and go to your profile by pressing your profile icon.
2. Tap *Followers*.
3. Find the account you want to block and tap the name.
4. Tap the gear icon and select *Block* or *Report*.

How to protect an account

If you don't want your tweets to be seen by the world, or you want more control over who follows you, you can use a Twitter feature that locks down the account so no one except your followers can see what you are tweeting.

If you are new to Twitter, protecting your account will make it very difficult to start conversations and gain followers. However, if you have a pressing reason to close your tweets to public view, follow these steps:

1. Go to *twitter.com* and log on.

2. Click your profile icon in the Twitter toolbar and select *Settings and privacy*.

3. Select the menu titled *Privacy and safety*.

4. Under Privacy, select the *Protect my tweets* option:

When you are done, click the *Save changes* button at the bottom of the page.

CHAPTER 4

Tweeting

You've created an account, and are now following other people on Twitter. It's time to start tweeting! This chapter explains how to send tweets, participate in discussions, and start discussions of your own.

How to create a tweet

Creating a new tweet is a cinch, and Twitter gives you multiple ways to do it.

Online:

Go to *twitter.com* and make sure you are logged in. Look for the *What's happening* field at the top of the screen, above your home timeline:

1. Place your cursor in the field, and start typing.

2. As you type, a counter below the field counts down how many characters you have left. Once you have typed 280 characters, the number will turn negative, meaning the tweet will be cut off unless you manually reduce the overage.

3. When you are ready to release your tweet to the world, click the *Tweet* button below the text-entry field.

There's another way to compose a new tweet. In the upper right corner of the browser window, next to your profile icon in the Twitter toolbar, is a *Tweet* button. Click it to write a new tweet.

Mobile app:

Twitter's mobile apps are also easy to use, although they will require you to use a smaller keyboard.

1. Find the Compose icon, which looks like a small button with a feather lying across it.

2. Use the keyboard or the dictation function on your device to create the tweet.

3. Tap the *Tweet* button when you are ready to send it.

Deciding what to tweet about

While creating a tweet is easy, deciding what to tweet about can be tricky for newcomers.

Writing great tweets will involve understanding your audience and seeing what works for them, while keeping true to your own style of communication. Sometimes it's helpful to look to other people for inspiration. However, as I explain later in this section, the tone of the conversation can change depending on who you follow. I also discuss how to get past mental blocks associated with using this new medium for the first time.

Finally, I have some practical tips about how to come up with great tweets to get the ball rolling.

What do other people usually tweet about?

What kinds of things do people tweet about? It really depends on who you follow. In Chapter 1, I showed you some individual examples of tweets by a famous person (@Oprah), a small business (@Momogoose), and several ordinary users. But if you follow hundreds of people, chances are you will see some patterns emerge, based on their interests.

For instance, if I were to use a phrase to describe the tweets from the hundreds of people I follow (a mix of journalists, tech/Web people, people from the Boston area, and random friends), it would be "observations about life, careers, and major events, with lots of overlap."

Here's another way to break it down:

Observations: People have interests, activities, and professional backgrounds, which will be reflected in their tweets. Someone has just finished a book, cooked a meal, attended a meeting, gone for a jog, or commented on the weather.

Major events: When there's a major event, such as a natural disaster, political scandal, or a splashy gadget release, a surge of topical tweets occurs as people I know react to or *retweet* the news (learn more about retweeting later in this guide). For instance, the night Apple co-founder Steve Jobs died, about half of the people I followed had something to say about it. National elections and the Olympics also bring out a lot of Twitter commentary.

Overlap: On any given weekend, many of the people I follow will be watching the same TV show or sporting event. Because I follow so many technology people, I see a lot of references to companies such as Google, Apple, and Microsoft.

But here's the thing: What I see on Twitter is not representative of what other people see. A fashionista in Manhattan will have a far different experience with Twitter, based on her interests and the people she follows. She will see more tweets and photos involving clothing, shoes, accessories, and sales, as well as more information specific to New York City.

A football fan in Florida is more likely to follow other football fans whose tweets include football references. A programmer living in Paris is more likely to see tweets about programming and his or her neighborhood in the 19th arrondissement. What about a hairdresser in Hollywood? Or a scientist in Singapore? They will follow different types of people, and will see and send different types of tweets.

Of course, you can follow the lead of other accounts and start tweeting about similar topics. But it's also possible to develop your own voice, as I describe below.

Mental blocks to tweeting

A lot of people feel strange using Twitter for the first time. "Why would any-one care about what I have to say?" is one comment I constantly hear from new users. Others feel slightly uncomfortable sharing information publicly, even if the information is not particularly sensitive or important. A few peo-ple complain that they don't have enough room to say what they want to say in just 280 characters.

Here are some responses to put your mind at ease:

"The stuff I have to say is too boring." Most people won't be particularly interested in the fact that your cat Mr. Elmer P. McFurrikins is curled up on the couch right now, and boy, doesn't he look cute?

But tweets about the mundane aspects of your life contain something that is vitally important to gaining followers and taking part in discussions: *authenticity.*

Tweets about the weather, the crowds at the mall, your kid's basketball game, and even your cat demonstrate that you are a real person, are proba-bly friendly, and are willing to share information about your life.

Considering the number of cat people in the world, I wouldn't be surprised if you got a response like this:

"280 characters aren't enough to say what I want to say!" I used to be like this. As a blogger accustomed to writing hundreds of words at a time, the idea of short bursts on Twitter seemed limiting. But I quickly learned that it's possible to say quite a bit in 280 characters. Observations can be brief, identifying key pieces of information:

When deep analysis or description is required, that's when posting photographs and links to long-form material comes in handy.

Lastly, Twitter teaches you to be spare with words. The character counter can inform you if a tweet is too long:

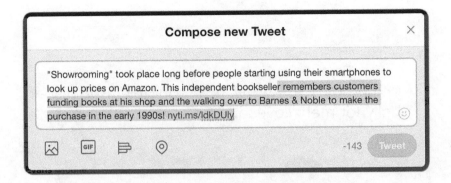

The tweet, which was more than twice as long as Twitter allows, was eventually reduced to a compact version that has 12 characters to spare:

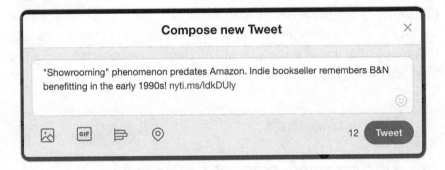

"I'm uncomfortable sharing information publicly." The idea of posting opinions, observations and random snippets of life for people (including complete strangers) to see can be a little unnerving at first.

For some, it's an unfamiliar concept. For others, there is a worry about tweeting something that might put them in a bad light. And then there are those who like the idea of tweeting, but get concerned that certain people might spot a specific tweet ("What will my boss/neighbor/ex-boyfriend think if they see the tweet I made on Saturday night?").

Finding your comfort level

With Twitter, keep in mind that *you don't have to share any more information than you want to share.* Here are tips for dialing things down to keep them at a level that makes you comfortable:

➤ Your Twitter handle does not have to reflect your actual name. If @bobcsmith22 is too revealing, change it to @bobbiec22 or @McTurtleman.

➤ You can remove elements from your Twitter profile, or use anonymous information. You don't have to use a real name. You can leave your location blank, and use a photo of your cat or dog instead of an actual profile photo.

➤ To reduce the chance of certain people seeing your tweets, avoid mentioning their names (which can appear in search engine results) or Twitter handles (which show up in their *Notifications* area) when you are tweeting.

➤ If you are about to tweet something that might be considered controversial or offensive, take some time to reflect on the contents of the tweet before posting it for others to see.

Controversial and angry tweets

On this last point, you can also use softer language. For instance, after seeing dog doo in the local park, you might be inclined to fire off an angry tweet:

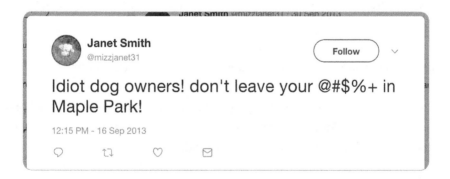

That's liable to rub *all* dog owners the wrong way. How about tweeting something that not only clarifies who is at fault, but also starts a constructive dialogue?

One final comment regarding controversial tweets: Check your employer's online communications policies before tweeting information or photos that may relate to your job. Many companies have guidelines that cover social media use by their employees.

Tips for writing great tweets

So you've gotten over your hang-ups about tweeting. Here's where the rubber hits the road—it's time to start tweeting! But what can you tweet about?

The obvious answer is "anything you feel comfortable sharing." I'm going to make it a little easier for you by suggesting a few ways to get those creative juices flowing.

Tip #1: What did you see/hear/experience in the last 24 hours that was notable?
It could have been a memorable play in last night's football game, the Chinese food you ate for lunch, the classic song you're listening to now, or the person dressed as a Yeti at the neighborhood parade:

Tip #2: What made you laugh out loud?

Humor is all around you. Colleagues, neighbors, children, and strangers will sometimes say or do something that makes you laugh. TV shows and other mass media are another source of laughter. These moments can be shared on Twitter. And, of course, one-liners are made for Twitter.

Tip #3: What tidbit would you share with friends, coworkers, or neighbors?

What sorts of information do you share in the real world? Do you have any personal updates or observations that could be shared publicly? It's a bad idea to share malicious or embarrassing gossip ("Did you see how plastered Dave was at the barbecue?"). However, other bits of neighborly news that you or other people might say aloud can be shared on Twitter.

Tip #4: What would you say on Facebook?

In many cases, information or observations you share on Facebook can be pasted directly into Twitter afterward. There are even Twitter applications that allow people to post to Facebook and Twitter simultaneously, without copying and pasting. On the official companion website for this guide (located at *twitter.in30minutes.com*) I have included a review of one such application, Hootsuite.

However, do not tweet information that's meant to stay in a closed conversation on Facebook. Remember, almost all tweets are public, whereas most Facebook posts are intended to be limited to a small group of people.

Tip #5: Share an interesting link

Sharing links on Twitter is a great way to spread news, videos, shopping deals, or useful online resources. It's easy to do, and Twitter automatically substitutes a shortened link to help keep your tweets below the 280-character limit.

You may notice that many articles, blogs, YouTube videos and websites have icons, buttons, and links to make tweeting easier:

If you click the button or link, it will allow you to share the headline and the link on Twitter. Regardless of whether you are on a desktop computer or smartphone, you may be prompted to log into Twitter to allow sharing of the link with followers.

You may also be able to edit the tweet before it goes out, but don't edit or delete the link itself. Press *Submit* to share the link.

You can also copy links from a web browser or email and paste them into a tweet, or retweet links posted by other people on Twitter.

Tip #6: Ask other people for help

Twitter is a great place to ask for advice. I'm not talking about serious, soul-searching questions ("Should I marry him?") but rather the quick questions that your followers or other Twitter denizens may be able to help with. For instance:

Tips for taking great photos

Photos are a great way to connect with followers. They're easy to post, too.

When you write a tweet on *twitter.com* or compose a tweet using the Twitter mobile app, you'll notice a photo icon near the text field:

Clicking or tapping the icon allows you to choose a photo to include in your tweet. The photo may already exist on your hard drive or mobile phone, or you can create a new one. Twitter will upload the photo to its servers when you post the tweet. The photo will be automatically displayed to those followers using *twitter.com* or the Twitter mobile app.

As you might expect, people like to share photos of interesting or beautiful sights, as well as food, pets, and family vacations. But I've also seen people using photos to illustrate a situation, such as a turkey hanging around a suburban highway:

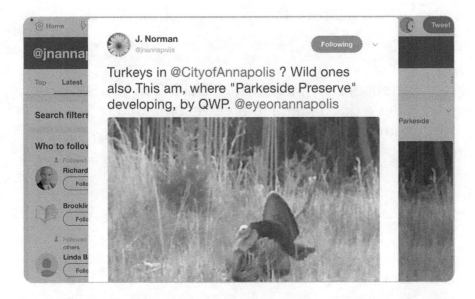

Unexpected or uncommon scenes tend to get noticed. A few years ago, I was on a flight that was aborted not long after takeoff. The pilot announced the aircraft would be dumping all of its fuel over the ocean before returning to the airport. Here's the photo I took and tweeted:

What photos should you share on Twitter? It depends on what you think is interesting … or what you think your audience will like. Try a few shots, and see how people react!

How to delete tweets

You've created a tweet. What if you want to get rid of it?

On the Web:

1. Go to *twitter.com* and your home timeline, showing the list of all of your tweets, with the newest tweets at the top of the list.

2. Find the tweet you want to delete. Look for the More icon (a downward-pointing arrow) and click it.

3. Select *Delete Tweet.*

4. You will be asked to confirm the deletion. Once you give your approval, the tweet is gone!

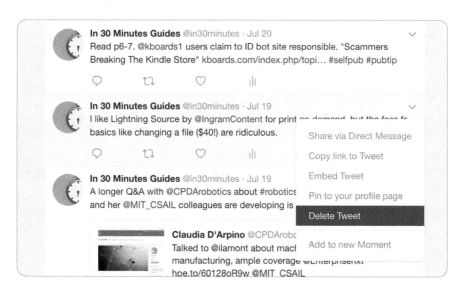

Phone or tablet:

1. Open the mobile Twitter app.

2. Go to your profile. This will show a list of your recent tweets.

3. Find the tweet you want to delete in the list of tweets, and tap the downward-pointing arrow next to the tweet.

4. Select *Delete*.

5. Confirm that you want to delete it.

The tweet will be removed from your timeline.

Regardless of which method you use to delete a specific tweet, it may still live on if it has been manually saved by someone else.

CHAPTER 5

Advanced Twitter: Joining the discussion

Twitter is not just about one-way tweets. It's possible to have conversations on Twitter with other people, and connect and share in other ways. We'll explore Twitter discussions in the following pages.

In addition, many Twitter users employ unfamiliar conventions, such as hashtags. Once you understand how the syntax works, you'll realize Twitter discussions mirror the ways in which humans have always shared information.

We'll also examine how a single tweet can reach thousands or even millions of people in a short period of time. Tweets that "go viral" can be incredibly informative, but can also spread incorrect information.

Someone responded to my tweet!

One day, in your *Notifications* area (look for the bell icon), you may see a response to one of your earlier tweets. Here's an example:

You can create an "@reply" (pronounced "at-reply") by clicking the *Reply* icon below a tweet. The icon looks like a tiny speech bubble.

Try it on any tweet in your home timeline. You'll see that Twitter automatically shows the Twitter handle of the person you are responding to. Then it's up to you to add additional text, which might be a comment or more information. Click the *Tweet* button to send your @reply.

Note that @replies won't be seen by other users unless they too follow the account that starts the tweet, or they are actively looking at all of the tweets from a specific account. So, if by some miracle @Oprah sent an @reply to one of your tweets, none of your followers would see it, unless they too were following @Oprah.

Why don't famous people respond to my tweets?

After releasing the first edition of this book, I received an email from a user who was puzzled: Why didn't well-known Twitter accounts ever respond to his tweets?

It's a fair question. Twitter is a great way to connect with people, and it's so easy to respond to a tweet.

However, actors, musicians, politicians, TV stars, and well-known organizations and brands live by a different set of rules on Twitter. Here are some reasons high-profile accounts seldom respond:

➤ The tweets from fans are hard to understand ("Loved that thing you said the other night at your concert! #LOL").

➤ The tweets are insulting ("You look like a pregnant cow on TV").

➤ The tweets ask questions which are difficult to answer in 280 characters ("What are your thoughts about Tibetan Buddhism?").

➤ When it comes to controversial issues, famous accounts don't want to take sides or make statements that might harm their public stature.

➤ Celebrities don't have enough time to reply to everyone.

Regarding this last point, while it's easy to send out a single tweet to a single fan, the math doesn't work for large numbers of fans. For instance, even if @Oprah took a break from promoting the latest Oprah's Book Club selection and decided to say "Hi!" to each one of her Twitter followers every minute of every day, it would take tens of thousands of years to get through the millions of people currently following her!

Someone mentioned me!

When browsing your notifications, you may notice tweets from other people that contain your Twitter handle, but are not responding to something you've tweeted about. Here's an example:

These are called @mentions (pronounced "at-mentions"). They often contain acknowledgements, questions, or some other piece of information that the person who created the tweet wants you to see.

For instance, every day scores of people @mention the Twitter handle of a Boston-based blog called Universal Hub, to ask a question, share a special photo, or draw the editor's attention to some piece of local news:

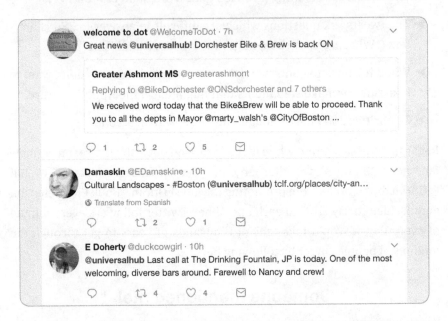

If you receive an @mention, it's up to you how to respond, such as by replying or retweeting. In many cases, no response is necessary.

Unfortunately, spammers and malicious hackers have latched onto @mentions. They know you will probably read a tweet that includes your Twitter handle. These spammers and hackers use @mentions to spread links to porn, coupon sites, and sites that install malware on visitors' computers. Be suspicious of click-bait that mentions your Twitter handle and includes a link to an unfamiliar website. If it's from an unknown Twitter account with a small number of previous tweets, it's probably spam.

Retweets

Retweet, *v. to repeat someone else's tweet, while giving credit to the original author; n. A tweet that has been copied and rebroadcast on another Twitter account, with the capital letters "RT" and the Twitter handle of the original sender added to the front of the new tweet.* You've just read my definition of a *retweet*, but an example should make the concept clear:

What's going on here? The Twitter user @estherschindler tweeted a humorous observation about everyday life. Another person, @RiCHi, thought the message was funny, and decided to repeat it using the letters "RT" (which means "retweet") and the original tweet.

It is no longer necessary to manually copy and paste a tweet or append "RT" and type the original poster's handle. It's much easier to click the Retweet icon below the original message, which looks like two arrows following each other. This automatically copies the handle of the author and the contents of the original tweet, and then posts it to your timeline.

It's also important to note that retweets allow you to acknowledge the original author. In the example above, if @RiCHi had simply copied the funny observation, but failed to credit the source, that's not a retweet. It's just copying.

Why do people retweet other people's tweets? Often, it's for the same reason that people might repeat what they heard from a friend, coworker, or neighbor—it's information, news, or a clever phrase that's worth repeating. It's also possible to retweet photos and news articles.

When using the retweet function on twitter.com, a pop-up will appear showing the original message. There is a field for adding an optional comment, but if you retweet it without a comment it will simply appear in your feed attributed to the original author.

The mobile app uses the same Retweet icon, but if you want to append a comment tap *Quote tweet* when prompted.

It is not possible to add a photo when using Twitter's retweet feature.

Hashtags explained

You may notice that some words in tweets are preceded by the hashtag symbol (#). Occasionally, there will be a hashtagged phrase or acronym with all of the spaces and periods removed. Hashtags are sometimes seen on advertisements or in television programs.

Hashtags are a Twitter convention that lets people easily find tweets about a certain topic. By adding a hashtag to the front of a word or phrase, it turns it into a link that points to Twitter's search engine. Click the link, and the most recent tweets that include the same hashtag are displayed. For example, here's what appeared when I clicked on *#RedSox*:

The *#RedSox* hashtag (and associated baseball-related hashtags, such as *#WorldSeries*) lets users see tweets from other fans, as well as news from various blogs and sports reporters. It's a very convenient way to connect with other like-minded Twitter users.

Hashtags serve other useful functions as well. They alert other Twitter followers to the fact that the tweet is about a certain topic that may not otherwise be apparent. For instance, let's say you're watching the Oscars on TV, and you see someone wearing a beautiful dress glide by the camera. You could ask your Twitter followers:

Followers not watching the program may not know what you are talking about. However, they will figure it out if you add an appropriate hashtag:

By adding *#oscars*, it's clear you are talking about the awards ceremony, and not something else. Moreover, anyone clicking on the *#oscars* link online or on their Twitter app will see all of the other tweets with the *#oscars* hashtag.

Sometimes people create funny hashtags. The late-night television host Jimmy Fallon and his writing team are especially skilled at this. They ask their viewing audience a funny question and then tell them to use a hashtag to let the writing team (and other viewers) see the answers. Here are some responses to his hashtag *#MisheardLyrics*:

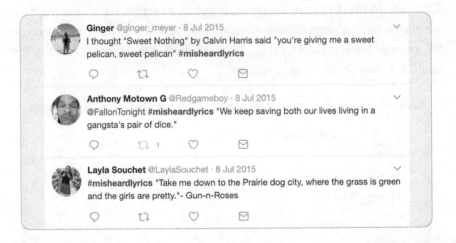

Hashtags are also used to reference sporting events (*#olympics*), fan groups (*#LakerNation*), political races (*#election2020*), conferences (*#ces2018*), and many other interests.

Practical uses for hashtags

Jimmy Fallon uses hashtags to communicate with his audience. Red Sox fans use hashtags to discuss their favorite team. Other people use hashtags to draw attention to specific topics, or to associate their tweets with places, concepts, and more.

Hashtags have additional uses:

1. **Adding a hashtagged topic to a question can help generate answers.** For example, if I wanted to ask my followers about the best Cuban restaurant in Miami, adding *#Miami* or *#cubanfood* to the end of my tweet would generate some additional eyeballs from people who follow that topic, but don't follow me.

2. **Hashtags are a way to catch the attention of companies, event organizers, journalists, and other people who have a strong interest in a certain topic.** I once attended an event that had its own hashtag, and used the hashtag in my tweets for an entire day. Later that day, I was introduced to the event organizer. He already knew who I was—he had been following the hashtag all day and had seen my tweets. Adding that hashtag to my tweets helped me make a stronger connection in the real world.

Hashtag no-nos

Some new Twitter users make the mistake of turning every word in their tweets into hashtags. Here's an example:

It's hard to read and irritating. It's also unnecessary—hashtagging common nouns, verbs and other words doesn't add any value or insights. Clicking *#up* or *#my* in Twitter will return a list of random tweets about all kinds of topics, rather than a focused list based on specific topics.

Another mistake: using the wrong hashtag. For instance, followers of the Boston Red Sox generally use *#redsox* to talk about their team, not *#bostonredsox* or *#sox*.

Mistakes can also happen when a single hashtag is used by two different groups of people. Check out *#gastro*. It's used by people who like gourmet food … as well as doctors and patients discussing gastrointestinal ailments:

Bottom line: Choose your hashtags carefully. If I am interested in using a particular hashtag in a tweet, I often search Twitter first to make sure it's the appropriate one to use.

Going viral

Twitter discussions and retweets can sometimes lead to a piece of news, a photo, or some other piece of information "going viral." Here's what it looks like:

This is a strange photo tweeted by the Central Intelligence Agency (yes, even spy agencies use Twitter). It includes a funny description that evokes images of spy pigeons flying over the Berlin Wall to carry out secret missions.

Below the photo, the circling arrows icon indicates that more than one thousand other Twitter accounts have retweeted or liked this photo. It is very unusual for a single tweet to be shared so widely, but if the information or image is special, it can go viral.

How does a viral tweet spread? Let's say you post a cute picture of your cat playing the piano. Maybe two of your followers retweet this piece of information. What happens then are some followers of those two friends retweet it again, then each of the retweets are again retweeted by *their* followers, and so on … kind of like the old shampoo commercial!

If it gets retweeted enough, eventually a celebrity, politician, major news organization, or some other widely followed or trusted source will retweet it, at which point thousands or even millions of people are retweeting the same piece of information in a short period of time.

When something goes viral, it can lead to more followers and publicity for the person who first tweeted the information.

But there is a dark side to going viral, too. What if the information is incorrect, someone tweets a hoax, or the piano-playing cat was photoshopped?

This is not a hypothetical situation. It has happened before, and not just with innocent pieces of information or funny cat photos. Let's say someone tweets a piece of juicy gossip. It snowballs, but later it turns out that the information was false. In extreme cases, people have had their deaths prematurely reported, or have been fingered for crimes they did not commit. By the time the truth comes out, reputations have been damaged. Oftentimes, the people who tweeted or retweeted the false information are very embarrassed.

Because of the potential for false or exaggerated information to spread virally through retweets, I advise people to be careful when retweeting details relating to crimes, disasters, scandals, or unconfirmed news items. People can be hurt when false rumors are retweeted. Check the news or some other reliable source first.

Advanced features

While we don't have enough time to cover all aspects of Twitter, there are a few additional features and tools you should be aware of. They include Direct Messages, Likes, Lists, and Shortcut Keys.

Direct Messages

Direct messages (also known as "DMs") are like text messages. This feature lets you send a message (or forward someone else's tweet) to another person, or a group of people. No one else can see the message except for the recipients. However, the sender and the recipient must be following each other on Twitter.

To see or send a direct message, go to your profile page and click the icon that looks like an envelope.

Likes

If you follow a lot of people, you may want to "like" certain tweets created by other accounts. Conversely, from time to time, other people may like tweets you've created. Some people use likes to bookmark tweets or links for follow-up, while others employ it to acknowledge interesting or good tweets. I sometimes like a tweet that mentions me to let the author know I have seen it.

To like a tweet, look for the heart icon below the tweet in question. Clicking it adds the tweet to your list of likes.

To see all of the tweets that you've liked, follow these steps:

1. Go to your profile on *twitter.com.*
2. Select *Likes.*

Lists

Lists are a way of organizing Twitter accounts. Here are some examples:

➤ A list of people in your hometown with Twitter accounts.

➤ People you work with.

➤ Famous bands who are on Twitter.

➤ Thought leaders in the real estate industry.

➤ Comedians on Twitter.

Viewing a list's timeline displays the recent tweets from the people on the list. Here's how to see the lists that you have created or have been assigned to:

1. Go to *twitter.com.*

2. Open your profile.

3. Select *Lists.*

You can create a new list and add an account to it by opening a profile page and clicking on the More Actions icon (three dots). Then, select *Add or remove from lists*:

You do not need to follow an account to add them to a list. In addition, public lists can be seen by anyone. In other words, if you create a list of Twitter accounts with funny profile pictures, not only will other people be able to see it, but the people you have added to the list will probably find it, too. To prevent this from happening, set the list to *Private.*

Shortcut keys

On *twitter.com,* shortcut keys are an easy way to perform common functions, such as creating a new tweet, replying, searching, or scrolling down. Press one of the following letters or symbols on the keyboard to activate the following functions:

➤ **N** – Create a new tweet.

➤ **J** – Select the first tweet in the timeline. Subsequent presses select the next tweet in line.

➤ **K** – Select the previous tweet.

➤ **T** – Retweet selected tweet.

➤ **R** – Reply to selected tweet.

➤ **Space bar** – Scroll down. This is a great way to rapidly view recent tweets in your timeline.

➤ **Forward slash** – Places the cursor in the search field.

There are about a dozen more shortcut keys for more obscure or advanced functions. If you are on *twitter.com,* simultaneously press the shift and question mark keys on your keyboard to see them all.

Conclusion

In 30 minutes, you've learned the basics of Twitter, from creating an account to taking part in discussions. You now have a foundation of knowledge and practical skills that you can use to make new connections, share information, and better understand the world around you.

While it feels good knowing how Twitter works and what you can do with it, to really get value from Twitter, you have to regularly use it. After setting up your account, you should follow at least a few dozen interesting accounts, using the advice I gave in Chapter 3. I've also added videos, blog posts, and other resources to the official book website (*twitter.in30minutes.com*). Click on the *Updates* link to sign up for chapter updates and other news about Twitter.

Then start tweeting. You don't have to be fanatical, but try creating at least two tweets per day. It will help you get comfortable with Twitter, and develop your own unique voice on Twitter. Regular tweeting also will help you attract followers and engage in discussions.

Be sure to ask questions if you need help—people on Twitter generally like to help new users. Make an effort to retweet other people's interesting tweets. If you see an opportunity to help someone out on Twitter, do it. It can be as simple as answering a question or showing support in some other way.

Lastly, I welcome any reader to connect with me on Twitter. My handle is @ilamont. If you mention this account on Twitter and let me know that you own *Twitter In 30 Minutes,* you will get a special Twitter shout-out and I will follow you back. You can also contact me via email at ian@in30minutes.com.

Thanks for purchasing *Twitter In 30 Minutes,* and I hope to see you soon on Twitter!

About the author

Twitter In 30 Minutes (3rd Edition) is authored by Ian Lamont, an award-winning business and technology journalist. He has written for more than a dozen online and print publications and served as the managing editor of *The Industry Standard*.

Lamont has written several In 30 Minutes® guides, including *Dropbox In 30 Minutes*, *Google Drive & Docs In 30 Minutes*, and *Excel Basics In 30 Minutes*. He is also the creator of the Lean Media framework.

He is a graduate of the Boston University College of Communication and MIT's Sloan Fellows Program in Innovation and Global Leadership.

Index

Introduction to Genealogy Basics In 30 Minutes

The following bonus chapter is the introduction to the award-winning Genealogy Basics In 30 Minutes, by author Shannon Combs-Bennett. To download the ebook or purchase the paperback, visit the book's official website, genealogy.in30minutes.com.

When I was a child, I liked to listen to my family share family stories. At six years of age, sometimes I would hide away, just out of eyesight, as the adults discussed a memory or a special someone from decades past. The tales were often exciting or funny. Others were serious or sad. The characters—so interesting! And they were all connected to me and my family!

I found out that my maternal grandmother's father was 61 years old when she was born. She said that when my great-grandfather was a child, he could recall holding his mother's hand, watching his older brothers in their Union blues marching off to fight in the Civil War. My imagination ran!

Fast forward a few decades, and my love of family stories has blossomed into a full-fledged career as a professional genealogist. Now, in addition to researching my own family history, I help other people learn more about their families' histories. This book is another way for me to help people learn about their ancestors and become effective stewards of their families' histories.

Why are people interested in family history?

People of all ages and backgrounds are flocking to the field of genealogy in ever-increasing numbers. What's behind the surge? I think the interest has always been there, but in recent years media and technology have changed the dynamics. Consider these factors:

➤ The widespread availability of inexpensive or free software for managing family records.

➤ Easier access to vital records and other data, thanks to online data-bases, social networks, and email.

➤ Television programs such as *History Detectives* and *Finding Your Roots*, which explain basic research concepts and share interesting genealogy stories involving famous people.

➤ Ever-present ads telling consumers how "easy" it is to trace your family tree.

Maybe you have seen the ads, or watched some of the TV programs. You may be very interested in learning about your own family tree. But where do you *really* start?

For me, genealogy is more than just a collection of names and dates. I went into the field because I want to know *who my ancestors were*. They may no longer be with us, but they are the reason I am here today. They were people, not just a bunch of names and dates listed in a dusty book or stored in a database. They had hopes, dreams, and needs, just as we all do. Through my research I am able to make connections, and watch personal stories unfold before me.

All kinds of people are interested in learning more about their roots. Do any of the following profiles seem familiar?

➤ **Sarah's grandmother always told her that the family came to North America on the *Mayflower*,** but no one ever seemed to believe the story. Curious, Sarah started to research her family history to see if her grandmother was right. Soon, she not only found one, but several *Mayflower* ancestors, and a fascinating family tree with roots across colonial New England. Thanksgiving now takes on a special meaning at her home. As she digs deeper into the family's history, the whole family loves learning about her discoveries.

➤ **John was adopted at birth and now wants to connect with his biological family.** Using what little information he knows about his origins, he has tried searching online and through paper records, but has not been able to find much. John has now turned to DNA testing with the hope that he can find a relative who will help him fill in his family tree and lead him to his birth parents.

➤ **Rose is of African-American heritage and wants to know more about the origins of her family.** Her grandparents did not talk much about growing up in Georgia, or about their extended families. Moreover, several records were destroyed in a house fire. Rose is certain that if she goes back far enough, she will find ancestors who were slaves. Nevertheless, she has a strong desire to know their stories.

➤ **David's father said the family's surname was changed at Ellis Island when their immigrant ancestor arrived in 1882.** After a visit to Ellis Island for a school trip, David discovered that the family legend was not supported by evidence in immigration records. Curious about why his great-grandfather, who was from Prussia, may have changed his name after arriving, David has begun to research his family history. He hopes one day he will be able to find records in Eastern Europe, where his family originated.

➤ **After Margaret's mother died, Margaret was cleaning out the attic.** She found a trunk full of letters, a family Bible, and old photographs. No one in the family recognizes the people in those photos, but Margaret noticed her mother's maiden name on the backs of several of the pictures. She has begun to reach out to cousins far and wide. One day she hopes to learn the identities of all of the people in the old photos, and where they came from.

Later, I will share more information about these cases. The names are not real, but the situations are based on real family research situations that can give you insights into your own genealogy quests.

What's in this guide

Genealogy has been around for hundreds of years in Europe. At first, it was a way for heralds to track noble families. At the end of the 19th Century, genealogy became a way for Americans to document their lineage—both Old World and Native American lines. In the 1970s, Alex Haley's *Roots* came to the small screen, energizing a new generation to seek out their family origins.

Genealogy is now booming. Thanks to an array of new tools and information sources, there has never been a better time to learn about your family's history. But the process can be daunting.

That's where this guide comes into play. This short guide will not only explain basic concepts and methods for family research, but it will also help you approach your research tasks in a smarter way that will save time and hopefully lead to better results. Topics include:

➤ The best approach to building a family tree and charting your research

➤ The most important records to look for

➤ Five things that can really trip up newbies (and tips for avoiding them)

➤ Dealing with "brick walls" in family research

➤ Approaching relatives for records, information, and family stories

➤ Research road trips, and what to bring in your portable genealogy kit

➤ The promise and perils of online research

➤ Getting started with genetic genealogy

➤ How to properly cite your findings

➤ Preserving family records and research for the next generation

We only have 30 minutes, so let's get started!

If you're interested in learning more about this title, or buying the ebook or paperback, visit the official website located at genealogy.in30minutes.com.

Introduction to Crowdfunding Basics In 30 Minutes

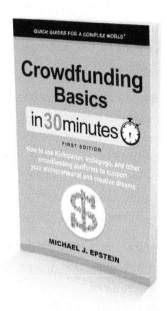

The following bonus chapter is the introduction to Crowdfunding Basics In 30 Minutes, by author Michael J. Epstein. To download the ebook or purchase the paperback, visit the book's official website, crowdfunding.in30minutes.com.

Just a few short years ago, if you wanted to start a business selling a new kind of bicycle or raise money to make an independent movie, you had no choice but to scrape together funding on your own or hope a generous friend or relative might be willing to put up seed capital. Now it is possible to look to the online masses and leverage crowdfunding, not only to raise money to fund your idea, but also to generate excitement and build a community of supporters. Crowdfunding is truly a game changer for those of us without easy access to capital for our projects!

Crowdfunding involves raising money through small contributions from a large number of people using online platforms. It has the potential to level the playing field for independent creators, entrepreneurs, and artists. Crowdfunding can also bring together communities, driving the pooling of resources to support people in need, to overcome bureaucratic or logistical obstacles, or to provide public benefit.

Crowdfunding is a powerful trend, and has wide-reaching implications. It has the potential to broaden grassroots support for new art, cutting-edge business concepts, and local causes, thereby weakening the hold of conservative gatekeepers who might otherwise be unwilling to risk supporting ideas that are too bold or innovative. There are now numerous crowdfunding services and accompanying support tools, making crowdfunding viable for an increasingly wide range of projects and causes, from the personal to the professional.

But crowdfunding is imperfect, and not every campaign is successful! For your campaign to reach its fundraising and project goals, a lot of hard work and careful planning will be required. You must consider the benefits and pitfalls of running a campaign and ensure that your enthusiasm is tempered with a realistic understanding of what crowdfunding can achieve. In the coming chapters, we'll take a look at whether crowdfunding is right for your project, and how you can maximize your chances for success.

The growth of crowdfunding

I became interested in crowdfunding in 2011 when I realized that it could help bring together a group of local artists to make an independent feature film. Because film is relatively unusual to the independent arts community in Boston, the idea was met with great enthusiasm. Now, five years later, I have not only used crowdfunding to grow a filmmaking career from scratch, but I have also consulted on dozens of film, theater, music, entrepreneurial, and cause-related crowdfunding projects.

In addition, I have backed more than 500 projects launched by other people on a dozen different crowdfunding platforms. Among these projects, I have seen massive successes and heartbreaking failures. These outcomes have provided important lessons in designing and executing crowdfunding campaigns, as well as working to fulfill promises to backers as projects are completed.

There has been exponential growth in crowdfunding over the past few years. Kickstarter has been leading the wave. Consider these Kickstarter statistics:

➤ More than 350,000 projects launched.

➤ More than 120,00 projects funded.

➤ Over 35 million individual pledges.

➤ Total pledges: more than $3 billion.

The population at large is now aware of crowdfunding as an alternate method for raising capital. With its widespread acceptance, crowdfunding could be the ticket to turning your great idea into a reality!

As familiarity and confidence spread, crowdfunding will continue on a growth trend for a long time to come. In fact, as traditional entertainment, manufacturing, retail, and publishing industries lose their monopolies on mainstream consumerism, opportunities for the crowdfunded creation of products will be ever more plentiful. It just might be the right time to look at crowdfunding for your project or cause.

Examples of great crowdfunding projects

While crowdfunding has become popular with celebrities and founders with significant fan and financial bases, the stories presented here will focus on creators with more modest resources. These examples serve as models for connecting enthusiastic niche communities with campaigns based on bold ideas or important needs. Crowdfunding is truly available to just about anyone with a great idea and a willingness to work hard to get it out there.

Consider the following examples:

➤ **Maxwell Bogue, Peter Dilworth, and Daniel Cowen created 3Doodler®, a 3D pen allowing artists to hand draw 3D objects.** Their two crowdfunding campaigns helped test the public's interest in their unique tool, leading not only to nearly $4 million in pledges, but the launch of a successful business.

➤ **Alice's dog Pepper has a serious, but treatable, medical condition that would result in a shortened lifespan without expensive surgery.** Alice's friends and family helped organize a crowdfunding campaign to raise the $5,000 necessary to cover Pepper's medical bills.

➤ **Jonathan wanted to create a large-scale, interactive art installation.** He crowdfunded Visualize Somerville, a multisensory, attendee-controlled art installation. This ephemeral experience allowed backers to not only support his project, but to also actively engage and become part of the creation itself.

➤ **Catherine, a songwriter and bandleader, had created a concept album celebrating historical and mythical women, but the project was incomplete.** She wanted to add a visual component to the project and had come up with the idea of producing a film anthology to accompany the songs. She raised money to hire 14 filmmakers from around the world to create the *Bring Us Your Women* film.

➤ **Every year, FamilyAid Boston sets up a crowdfunding campaign for volunteer runners taking part in the Boston Marathon.** Runners and their supporters solicit pledges that are used by the organization to help homeless families find housing. Last year, the campaign raised more than $100,000.

➤ **Alexandria turned to a crowdfunding patronage system to support her projects.** Backers pay a small amount of money at a regular interval, or when she creates something new. This allows her to focus on doing video and photo shoots to showcase her costume creations.

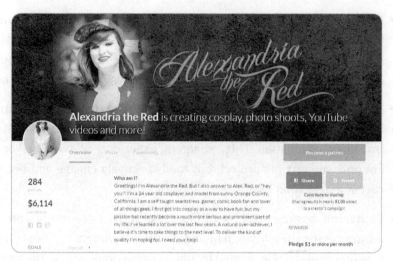

➤ **Roger was a journalist looking to write a historical piece about the use of certain technologies in Cold-War-era espionage.** There was great interest in the story from several publications and from the public, but his budget was too limited to thoroughly investigate without additional support. Roger raised money via crowdfunding to file Freedom of Information Act requests and to travel to primary sources to gather information for his story.

The scope and goals of these projects may have been different, but each one attracted a group of backers to help overcome financial and logistical hurdles to transform an otherwise impossible dream into a successful reality. Moreover, backers were empowered to be part of bringing the creator's ideas to fruition.

How can crowdfunding work for you?

Now that you have read a few success stories, you may be wondering if crowdfunding could work for your concept. This book will not only explain how crowdfunding works, it will also show the practical steps involved in running a campaign:

➤ In Chapter 1, we will examine the philosophical and logistical differences between crowdfunding and traditional funding, before breaking down the types of projects well-suited for crowdfunding efforts.

➤ Chapter 2 is all about planning, from choosing the right platform to setting up a realistic budget.

➤ Chapter 3 discusses the preparation of promotional materials and explains how to set up reward tiers for backers.

➤ In Chapter 4, we will explore communication tactics, including press outreach and methods for keeping backers engaged.

➤ Chapter 5 covers post-campaign activities, from keeping backers informed about the progress of your project to distributing rewards.

By the time we finish, you will be well on your way to running your own crowdfunding campaign. We only have 30 minutes, so let's get started!

If you're interested in learning more about this title, or buying the ebook or paperback, visit the official website located at crowdfunding.in30minutes.com.

Notes

CPSIA information can be obtained
at www.ICGtesting.com
Printed in the USA
LVHW011526311018
595484LV00012B/234/P